Twelve Colorful Things

by Heather Tietz

illustrated by Nancy Miller

Ambassador
Children's Books
Mahwah • New Jersey

To Nana and Papa and Grandma and Grandpa, for the countless, colorful things you have brought into my children's lives. — H.T.

To my dear friend Pat who taught me how to knit. — N.M.

Book and jacket design by Jennifer Conlan

Text copyright © 2011 by Heather Tietz
Art copyright © 2011 by Nancy Miller

Library of Congress Control Number: 2010940387

ISBN: 978-0-8091-6752-4

Published by Ambassador Books
An imprint of Paulist Press
997 Macarthur Boulevard
Mahwah, New Jersey 07430

www.ambassadorbooks.com

Printed and bound in Shenzhen, China
by Shenzhen Donnelley Printing Co. Ltd.
February 2011

For God loves a cheerful giver.
— *2 Corinthians 9:7*

January

One lonely lady,
one wooden chair,
one creaky porch,
one empty stair,

one crowded treehouse,
one perfect plan,
one year of gifts,
made with their hands.

February

Two clever cupids,
two arrows shine,
aimed at her mailbox:
pink valentines!

March

Three green goodies
from lively leprechauns.

April

Four purple peepers
hatching in her lawn.

May

Five dozy bundles
beneath the silver moon.

June

Six yellow sunshines
in bountiful, bursting bloom.

July

Seven marching songs
red, blue, and starry white.

August

Eight golden tales
aglow with firefly light.

September

Nine caramel apples
drippy, sticky,
sweet, and brown.

October

Ten orange pumpkins
tipsy,
topsy,
upsy down.

November

Eleven painted pots soil black as night,
eleven sleepy seeds waiting for sunlight.

December

Twelve brilliant bulbs twinkle in her tree.
Eleven pretty pots sit patiently.
Ten pumpkin pies cool in the shade.
Nine apple seeds sit on a spade.
Eight summer stories open by the bed.
Seven marching songs parade through her head.

Six dried flowers wrapped round a wreath.
Five dark bundles snuggle down to sleep.

Four mother hens roost by her door,
three cookie crumbs lay on the floor,
two valentines brighten up her shelf,
one well-loved lady hums to herself.

Soft snow is falling.
Winter has come.
Two knitting needles
finally are done.

One little lady has a secret, too.
Tight goes a ribbon on a package made for two.
With bounce in her step, she bundles head to toe.

She has twelve colorful things
for two children in the snow.